# Child's Guide to Reconciliation

BY Elizabeth Ficocelli

Illustrations by Anne Catharine Blake

PAULIST PRESS
New York/Mahwah, N.J.

For my sons,

Michael, Nicholas, Daniel, and Matthew,

who keep me confessing often

E. F.


For my daughter, Lady Lightning,

also known as Amanda Kay Henze

A. C. B.

Caseside design by Sharyn Banks
Caseside illustrations by Anne Catharine Blake

Text copyright © 2003 by Elizabeth Ficocelli

Text illustrations copyright © 2003 by Anne Catharine Blake

Library of Congress Cataloging-in-Publication Data

Ficocelli, Elizabeth.
    Child's guide to Reconciliation / by Elizabeth Ficocelli; illustrations by Anne Catharine Blake.
        p. cm.
    Summary: Provides guidance on receiving the sacrament of Reconciliation for the first time, describing the purpose and procedure of the rite and why it is a reason to celebrate.
    ISBN 0-8091-6709-3 3078 3848 9/04
    1. Penance—Juvenile literature. 2. Forgiveness—Religious aspects—Catholic Church—Juvenile literature. 3. Reconciliation—Religious aspects—Catholic Church—Juvenile literature.
    [1. Penance. 2. Reconciliation. 3. Sacraments—Catholic Church. 4. Catholic Church.] I. Blake, Anne Catharine, ill. II. Title.
    BX2260.F48 2003
    264′.02086—dc21
                                                                                    2003010259

Published by Paulist Press
997 Macarthur Boulevard
Mahwah, New Jersey 07430

www.paulistpress.com

Printed and bound in Mexico

*My name is*

_____

*I celebrated Reconciliation for the first time on*

_____

*Helping me celebrate were*

_____

_____

_____

Hi! My name is Clare. This year my classmates and I have been learning about God's love and forgiveness. God is always ready to forgive us. All we have to do is ask. A very special way to ask for God's love and forgiveness is the *Sacrament of Reconciliation*. Reconciliation means to be friends again.

This is an important day for me. I'm about to receive the Sacrament of Reconciliation for the first time. And that's a reason to celebrate!

**Besides Clare, who else is celebrating God's forgiveness today?**

In class, Mrs. McClellan had us draw pictures about God's forgiveness. Emilio drew a picture of Jesus helping a blind man to see. Jennifer drew Jesus helping two people to be friends again. Raj drew a picture of Jesus hugging children and teaching them to pray. Everywhere Jesus went, he taught people to love God and each other.

That's what God wants *us* to do, too.

**Can you find the Bible story for each example of God's forgiveness?**

To help us, God gave us a special set of rules called the *Ten Commandments*. These rules help us make good and loving choices and live a happy life. We made a banner in our classroom to help us remember these rules.

Try to match the commandment with the right picture.

1. Love God with all your heart.

2. Use God's name with respect and love.

3. Keep Sundays special and holy.

4. Love and obey your mother and father.

5. Treat God's creations kindly.

6. Respect your body as a gift from God.

7. Don't take things that don't belong to you.

8. Always tell the truth.

9. Don't be jealous or greedy.

10. Help others who are in need.

Sometimes, even with these good rules to follow, we can forget what Jesus taught us. Did you ever do something that made you feel sorry?
    I have.

When that happens, I feel small and lonely and not very happy.

**How do you feel?**

When we choose not to love each other like Jesus wants us to, it's called a *sin*. A sin is not a mistake or an accident. Mistakes and accidents are not done on purpose. A sin is something we choose, even though we know it's wrong. Sin hurts our friendship with God and each other. It pulls us away from God's family.

**Which of these pictures is a mistake? An accident? A sin? Why?**

When I say I'm sorry to someone I've hurt, and do something nice for them, I feel much better. Now I need to make it better with God.

Mrs. McClellan read us a story from the Bible about God's forgiveness.
*Once there was a father who had two sons. One day, the younger son asked for his share of the family's money so he could go out on his own. The father agreed.*

The son left home and spent all his money on wasteful things. Soon, he was hungry and lonely and sorry for what he had done. He realized he had sinned against God and his father. He decided to go home. As he was on the road, his father saw him and was so happy that he gave the son a robe, a ring, sandals, and a big party to celebrate his return.

We are like the younger son. Sometimes we think about what *we* want, and not what *God* wants. God is like the loving and forgiving father. He will always be there to welcome us back when we ask.

**What are some things *we* want that God might not want for us?**

Now that I've learned how much God wants to forgive me when I turn away from him, I'm ready to receive the Sacrament of Reconciliation.

My friend Leon is next in line. He goes into a small room called the *confessional.* Our class visited the confessional together, so I know what it's like. Inside, there's a little kneeler, with a screen in front of it. On the other side of the screen, there's a chair for our priest, Father Chuck. Across from him there's an empty chair. You can kneel on the kneeler or you can sit in the chair facing the priest. It's up to you.

**Why might someone want to use the kneeler?**
**Why might someone want to use the chair?**

While I'm waiting, I try to remember things I've said or done that hurt someone else. This is called an *Examination of Conscience*. My Mom and Dad helped me with this at home. They told me to ask the Holy Spirit to help me remember my sins. They told me that we all do things we wish we hadn't. The important thing is that God will forgive us, every time!

**What kind of hurtful things might Clare be remembering? Have you hurt others? How?**

**Remember—God loves you and is ready to forgive you right now!**

I start to feel a little nervous, but then I remember that Father Chuck is my friend. He's not there to scold me or punish me. He's there to listen and help me. He's there to give me God's forgiveness!

It's my turn now. I go inside the confessional and sit on the chair facing Father Chuck. Father Chuck gives me a big smile. "Hello, Clare," he says. "I'm so glad you came today to celebrate God's forgiveness! I know God is happy, too. Let's begin now by praying together *in the name of the Father, and of the Son, and of the Holy Spirit.*"

I make the Sign of the Cross. Father Chuck reads a passage from the Bible about Jesus forgiving a woman for her sins. I remember that story from class. I feel happy for the woman. I know God will forgive me, too.

I tell Father Chuck that this is my first *confession*. A confession is when we talk to the priest about our sins. A priest is not allowed to tell anyone else what he hears in confession. So I can talk to Father Chuck about anything.

**With your finger, trace the Sign of the Cross on Clare.**

Father Chuck listens. He understands. He remembers feeling the same way when he was my age. We talk about how I can make changes so I can be a better follower of Jesus. Then Father Chuck gives me a *penance*. A penance is something we do to help make up for what we did wrong and to help us not do it again. Sometimes it may be a prayer. Sometimes it may be an action. My penance is to share the peace and love of Jesus by inviting someone else to the Sacrament of Reconciliation.

**Name a penance that's a prayer. Name a penance that's an action.**

I tell God I'm sorry for hurting my friendship with him. I pray an *Act of Contrition* that tells God I want to change. I can use my own words, but today I say a prayer we learned in class:

My God, I am sorry for my sins with all my heart. In choosing to do wrong and failing to do good, I have sinned against you whom I should love above all things. I firmly intend, with your help, to do penance, to sin no more, and to avoid whatever leads me to sin.

Now it's time for the *Absolution*, the words of God's forgiveness. Father Chuck places his hand on my head and gives me God's blessing. He tells me to go in peace.

I feel wonderful! I leave the confessional and smile at my family and friends waiting on line. I'm happy to be close to God's family again.

Being forgiven is a great feeling, and so is knowing that I can receive the Sacrament of Reconciliation any time I want to! Why don't *you* come and experience God's love and forgiveness too?

**If you haven't yet received Reconciliation, when will you receive it? If you have, when will you go next?**